10.5.77

# THE
# MAPLE HARVEST
# COOKBOOK

# THE MAPLE HARVEST COOKBOOK

## by Diane Lewis

*Illustrated by Jeff Parker*

STEIN AND DAY/*Publishers*/New York

First published in 1977
Copyright © 1977 by Diane Lewis
All rights reserved
Printed in the United States of America
Stein and Day/*Publishers*/Scarborough House,
Briarcliff Manor, N.Y. 10510

*Library of Congress Cataloging in Publication Data*

Main entry under title:

The maple harvest cookbook.

    Includes index.
    1.   Cookery (maple sugar and syrup)   I.   Lewis
Diane, 1944-
TX767.M3M36       641.6'3'6       77-22760
ISBN 0-8128-2201-3
ISBN 0-8128-2200-5 pbk.

Canadian material prepared by Elizabeth Hemsworth.

Sayings from *The Old Farmer's Almanac* are used by kind permission of Yankee, Inc.
of Dublin, New Hampshire

# Contents

1592344

## Especially Nice for Christmas Giving

*"To Everything There Is a Season"*

*Ecclesiastes III*

# Introduction

Welcome to our "Maple Harvest Cookbook," a collection of old and new recipes for maple cookery from the New England area. We hope you'll discover the delight of cooking with maple products and the special flavor that they bring to all of your family's meals.

Some of our restaurant's favorite recipes are included and marked with asterisks. We cook with a Grade C syrup and recommend it for the best results in your own use of the recipes; should you have Grade B on hand, however, it will serve almost as well. Our other recommendation is that you use a Fancy or Grade A syrup for candies as the flavor obtained is light and delicate. Since we have some recipes calling for maple sugar as an ingredient, we have included a recipe for making the sugar so that you may have it on hand; you'll find it in the "Candies" chapter.

And finally, we should like to extend a special "thank you" to friends who offered us their family recipes and cookbooks from the past so that we could bring to light some of New England's oldest and finest methods of cooking with Mother Nature's maple harvest.

*The Parker Family*
*Parker's Maple Barn*
*Mason, New Hampshire*

# From Sap to Syrup

*The Sugarmakers.* America's earliest sugarmakers were the Indians who in turn showed their Pilgrim neighbors the methods for tapping and boiling maple sap. To these newly arrived settlers it must have seemed a luxury to use the syrup and "sugar cakes" in their simple cooking rather than depend on the expensive cane sugar from overseas. In time they also used the maple products as bartering foods; it was a lucky household that had a large sugarbush for tapping come February. But, as with their Indian friends, they were in for some hard work before their syrup was ready.

Wooden spouts had to be carved and wooden buckets fitted together from the farm's forest. A team of horses or oxen was hitched to a handmade sled with gathering vessels on it for the trek to and from the sugarbush. When the sap reached home it had to be boiled over fires fed by hand-cut cords of wood chopped and dried long before the season started. Without cooking thermometers it was difficult to determine just when sap became syrup except through trial and error; only an experienced eye could judge that real syrup "aproned off" a wooden ladle in a wide sheet. The sugaring process was a difficult one for the early settlers but worth the effort to the families who loved what the Indians came to call "sweetwater."

In the early 1900s the sugarmaker's job became easier with the introduction of galvanized buckets and spouts, along with reliable thermometers. Warped and splitting buckets were a thing of the past, and determining sap temperatures was no longer a problem. Trucks and tractors replaced animal teams, making the collection of sap a speedier process. But although the sugarmaker used more efficient methods he still had to (and still does) work with Mother Nature as a "partner," and she will never be "modern" enough to tell him when the sap will rise or how much to expect!

*The Sap.* Around the middle of February the sugarmaker begins to study the weather and his thermometer. He is waiting for just the right temperatures—cold nights and sunny above-freezing days—to draw the sap up the maples. A sugar season lasts anywhere from four weeks to a bountiful month and a half, so he wants to tap at the right time in either case. He will finally judge to the best of his knowledge just which day is the right one and the adventure begins. He and his crew will load trucks with spouts and buckets and head out to the countryside to be greeted as the first harbingers of spring.

The crew must work as quickly as possible to get the buckets onto the trees, as no one yet knows how long the season will be. The first steps are to bore the holes, put in the spouts, and hang the buckets. Today's sugarmakers generally use a power drill to bore the holes and can do several hundred trees in two or three days. A tree of about 8" in diameter is the smallest tappable maple and only one bucket goes on it. For each 6" more of diameter another bucket can be added; the taps are bored at least 18" apart from one another. In the last few years many sugarmakers have installed plastic tubing (connected to plastic spouts) and run it in a continual line from tree to tree in a downhill direction. The sap can then flow directly to a gathering tank. Not only does this eliminate the emptying of several hundred buckets a day, but it allows tapping on the mountainsides where collection would be impossible in deep snow or ice.

The Syrup. Whether the sap is collected in buckets or through tubing, it is accumulated in large tanks where it's stored until it is ready to be brought to the sugarhouse. When it reaches the sugarhouse, it is transferred into large holding tanks and then fed into an evaporator. It is here that the syrup is produced.

The evaporator does just what its name implies—it evaporates water from the sap until syrup is obtained. It is fired by wood, oil, or gas to keep the sap boiling. The sap will become syrup when it is boiled up to a temperature of 7°F above the boiling point of water at the sugarmaker's altitude.

New Hampshire state law requires that maple syrup sold commercially must contain 67% sugar. Canadian law will soon require that maple syrup have a minimum 66% sugar content (up from 65%). However, too much sugar may cause the syrup to crystallize in the container. Therefore, a sugarmaker must use an instrument known as an hydrometer to measure the sugar content or density of his syrup. At the beginning of the season the sugar content of the sap is at its highest, which means that only about 20 gallons of sap are needed to make one gallon of syrup with the 67% sugar requirement. As the season progresses, however, the sugar content of the sap falls to a point where 40 to 50 gallons of sap are needed for that one gallon of syrup.

A second law requires that syrup be graded according to its color. The U.S. grades are classified as follows:

| GRADE | COLOR | FLAVOR |
|---|---|---|
| Fancy | Light Amber | Very light and mild |
| A | Medium Amber | Mellow |
| B | Dark Amber | Hearty |
| C | Very Dark Amber | Robust |

Quebec's five grades are AA, A, B, C, and D, ranging from the lightest (AA) to the darkest (D).

After the syrup's grade and density are calculated, it is fed through filters to eliminate excess calcium deposits and then poured into containers for sale or use. Syrup must be poured to the very tops of the bottles to prevent air from entering and forming mold. Some sugarmakers use a portion of the syrup to make maple sugar, candy, and maple cream.

Even when the last gallon of syrup has been capped, the sugarmaker's work is not really finished. During the months that follow March he may discuss new and better ways to fire his evaporator or improve his packaging. He may want to buy new drilling equipment or search out more maples to tap in the coming season. For him the season never really ends. Nor does it end for the lucky few who have syrup left right up until January and can pour Spring right out of a bottle!

In the recipes that follow, please note that the abbreviation "tea." has been used for teaspoon and the abbreviation "tbs." has been used for tablespoon. These were employed in place of the conventional abbreviations which are sometimes confused.

# Good Morning!

*But hark, I hear the Pancake-Bell,*
*And fritters make a gallant smell!*

*Old Song*

## Maple Corn Bread

| | | | | |
|---|---|---|---|---|
| 1 | egg, beaten | | 1 | cup cornmeal |
| 1/2 | cup milk | | 1 | cup flour |
| 3/4 | cup maple syrup | | 1/2 | tea. salt |
| 1/4 | cup soft butter | | | |

Preheat oven to 425°. In a large bowl beat together the egg, milk, syrup and butter. Sift together the cornmeal, flour and salt; add to the egg mixture and mix well. Bake in greased 8" pan for 20 minutes, or until done. Yields 9-12 squares.

## Maple Syrup Donuts

| | | | | |
|---|---|---|---|---|
| 1 | cup maple syrup | | 1/2 | tea. nutmeg |
| 2 | eggs, beaten | | 1 | tea. vanilla |
| 3 | Tbs. shortening | | 2/3 | cup milk |
| 1/2 | tea. salt | | 4-5 | cups of flour to work dough |
| 1 | tea. baking soda | | | |

Mix together all ingredients, except flour, in a large bowl. Batter should be smooth. Add enough flour, one cup at a time, until dough is workable and not too sticky. <u>Pat</u> it out on a floured board to 1/2" thickness and cut with a floured donut cutter (or glass rim). Heat fat to 370° and fry donuts until done on both sides. Yields 1 1/2-2 dozen donuts.

## Maple Biscuits

your favorite biscuit dough
maple syrup

chopped nuts
light cream

Mix up your favorite biscuit recipe in the usual amount. Pour 1/2" of maple syrup into your baking vessel. Add nuts and stir mixture. Place uncooked biscuits on top and cook as long as your recipe states. Take biscuits out of oven and serve upside down with light cream poured on top. They are best served warm.

## Maple Sugar Muffins

| | | | | |
|---|---|---|---|---|
| 2 | cups flour | 1 | egg, beaten |
| 3 | tea. baking powder | 1/4 | cup shortening |
| 1/2 | tea. salt | 1 | cup milk |
| | | 1/2 | cup maple sugar |

Preheat oven to 400°. Into a large bowl sift together the flour, baking powder and salt. Add the egg, shortening, milk and maple sugar and mix together well. Fill greased muffin tins 2/3 full and bake for 15 minutes, or until done. Yields about 1 dozen muffins.

## Squash Muffins

| | | | |
|---|---|---|---|
| 1/2 | cup milk | 2 | tea. melted butter |
| 1/2 | cup squash | 2 | Tbs. maple sugar |
| 1 | egg | 1 | cup flour |
| 1/4 | tea. salt | 2 | tea. baking powder |

Preheat oven to 350°. In a large bowl mix first 6 ingredients until well blended. Sift together the flour and baking powder and add to the mixture, mixing well. Spoon into greased muffin tins and bake for 30 minutes, or until done. Yields 1 dozen muffins.

## Coffee Nut Muffins

| | | | |
|---|---|---|---|
| 2 2/3 | cups flour | 1 | cup nuts, chopped |
| 4 | tea. baking powder | 1 | egg |
| 3/4 | cup maple sugar | 1 1/4 | cups cold black coffee |
| 1/2 | tea. salt | 2 | Tbs. melted shortening |

Preheat oven to 400°. Sift first four ingredients together; stir in nuts. In a large bowl beat together the egg, coffee and shortening. Add the dry ingredients and mix only enough to dampen all the flour. Bake in greased muffin tins about 20 minutes, or until done. Yields 2 dozen muffins.

14

## Spicy Muffins

| | | | | |
|---|---|---|---|---|
| 1/2 | cup shortening | 1/2 | tea. salt |
| 1/2 | cup maple sugar | 1 | tea. cinnamon |
| 1 | egg | 1 | tea. ginger |
| 1 | cup maple syrup | 1/2 | tea. cloves |
| 3 | cups sifted flour | 1 | cup hot water |
| 1 1/2 | tea. baking soda | | |

Preheat oven to 375°. Cream together shortening and sugar. Beat in the egg, then the syrup. Sift together the dry ingredients; stir into the syrup mixture. Gradually add hot water, beating until smooth. Line muffin pans with paper cups; fill 2/3 full. Bake for 20 minutes, or until done. Yields 2 dozen muffins.

## Sour-Cream Muffins

| | | | | |
|---|---|---|---|---|
| 2 | Tbs. butter | 4 | tea. baking powder |
| 1/4 | cup maple sugar | 1/4 | tea. salt |
| 2 | eggs | 1/4 | tea. baking soda |
| 2 | cups flour | 1 | cup sour cream |

Cream together the butter and sugar until the mixture is fluffy. Beat in eggs and mix well. Sift together flour, baking powder and salt. Dissolve baking soda in the sour cream and add to the creamed mixture alternately with the dry ingredients, beating until very fluffly. Spoon into well greased muffin cups and bake in a 425° oven for 15 minutes, or until done. Yields 1 1/2 dozen muffins.

## Maple Muffins*

| | | | |
|---|---|---|---|
| 2 | cups flour | 1/4 | cup shortening |
| 3 | tea. baking powder | 1/2 | cup milk |
| 1/2 | tea. salt | 1/2 | cup maple syrup |
| 1 | egg, beaten | | |

Preheat oven to 400°. In a large bowl sift together the flour, baking powder and salt. Add the egg, shortening, milk and maple syrup and mix well. Fill greased muffin tins to 2/3 full. Bake for 20 minutes, or until done. Yields 1 dozen muffins; recipe may be doubled.

## Maple All-Bran Muffins

| | | | |
|---|---|---|---|
| 1 | cup All-Bran | 1/3 | cup maple syrup |
| 3/4 | cup milk | 1 | cup flour |
| 2 | Tbs. melted shortening | 3 | tea. baking powder |
| 1 | egg, beaten | 1 | tea. salt |

Preheat oven to 400°. In a large bowl stir All-Bran and milk together. Add shortening, egg and syrup and mix well. Sift flour, baking powder and salt together and add to the mixture. Stir well. Spoon into greased muffin tins and bake for 15 minutes, or until done. Yields about 1 1/2 dozen muffins.

## Maple Corn Muffins

Sift together:
| | |
|---|---|
| 1 | cup flour |
| 3/4 | cup corn meal |
| 1/2 | tea. baking soda |
| 1/2 | tea. salt |

Make a batter of:
| | |
|---|---|
| 3/4 | cup milk |
| 1/4 | cup sour cream |
| 1/3 | cup maple syrup |
| 2 | eggs |

Preheat oven to 450°. Combine both mixtures together and bake in greased muffin tins for 15 minutes, or until done. Yields about 1 1/2 dozen muffins.

## Maple Fritters

| | |
|---|---|
| 4 | cups flour |
| 2 | tea. baking powder |
| 1/2 | tea. salt |
| 2 | cups milk |

| | |
|---|---|
| 1 | Tbs. light cream |
| 3 | eggs, beaten |
| 1 | cup <u>warm</u> maple syrup |
| | powdered sugar |

Set deep fat fryer at 350°. Sift flour, baking powder and salt together in a large bowl. Add milk and cream and stir together well. Add beaten eggs, stirring constantly. Drop by spoonfuls into hot fat and fry on both sides until puffed and brown. Drizzle warm syrup over warm fritters and sprinkle with powdered sugar. Serve warm. Yields 2-3 dozen fritters.

## Streusel Coffeecake

| | | | | |
|---|---|---|---|---|
| 3 | cups sifted flour | | 3 | Tbs. instant coffee |
| 3 | tea. baking powder | | 1/2 | cup butter |
| 1/4 | tea. salt | | 1/2 | cup shortening |
| 1 1/4 | tea. cinnamon | | 1 | cup milk |
| 1 | cup white sugar | | 1/8 | tea. baking soda |
| 1 | cup maple sugar, packed | | 2 | eggs |

*Preheat oven to 350°. Lightly grease and flour a 9" tube pan. In a large bowl sift flour, baking powder, salt, cinnamon, sugars and coffee. Using a pastry blender cut butter and shortening into flour mixture until it resembles small peas. Set aside 1 cup for topping. Combine milk with baking soda and eggs; mix well. With wooden spoon, stir all at once into flour-fat mixture just until combined. Turn into tube pan. Sprinkle evenly with reserved flour-fat mixture. Bake 50 minutes, or until done. Let cool 10 minutes and then remove from pan; serve warm. Serves 6-8.*

## Good Morning Marmalade Bread

| | | | | |
|---|---|---|---|---|
| 2 1/2 | cups sifted flour | | 3 | eggs, beaten |
| 1 | Tbs. baking powder | | 1 | cup orange marmalade |
| 1 | tea. salt | | 1 | Tbs. grated orange peel |
| 1/2 | cup maple syrup | | 1 | cup finely chopped walnuts |
| 2 | Tbs. soft butter | | | |

*Preheat oven to 350°. Grease a 9"x5"x3" loaf pan. Sift flour with baking powder and salt; set aside. In a medium bowl beat maple syrup, butter, and eggs until smooth. Stir in marmalade and orange peel, mixing well. Add flour mixture, stirring until well combined. Stir in nuts. Turn into pan; bake about 1 hour, or until done. Let cool in pan for 10 minutes; remove from pan and cool thoroughly. To serve, cut into thin slices.*

# Breads

*"Do not let the women fret for want of oven wood.
I hope that sister Tabatha will pay all attention to the bread trough.
I cannot bear to eat lead and clay when good, sweet, light bread
is just as easily made."*

*Farmer's Almanac, 1811*

## Cheese and Herb Bread

| | | | |
|---|---|---|---|
| 2 | cups of warm water | 1/2 | cup plus 1 Tbs. grated |
| 2 | pkgs. active dry yeast | | Parmesan cheese |
| 2 | Tbs. maple sugar | 1 1/2 | Tbs. dried oregano leaves |
| 2 | tea. salt | 4 1/4 | cups sifted all-purpose flour |
| 2 | Tbs. soft butter | | |

Sprinkle yeast over water in large bowl. Let stand a few minutes; stir to dissolve. Add sugar, salt, butter, 1/2 cup cheese, oregano, and 3 cups of flour. Beat with electric mixer at low speed until blended. At medium speed, beat until smooth—for 2 minutes. With a wooden spoon gradually beat in rest of flour. Cover with waxed paper and towel. Let rise in warm place free from drafts about 45 minutes, or until more than double in bulk. Meanwhile, preheat oven to 375°. Lightly grease a 1 1/2 or 2 quart casserole; set aside. With a wooden spoon stir down the batter. Beat hard for 1/2 minute. Turn into casserole. Sprinkle top of batter evenly with 1 Tbs. cheese. Bake 50 minutes, or until browned. Turn out immediately onto wire rack. Serve slightly warm.

## Toasted Bread

| | | | |
|---|---|---|---|
| 9 | slices white bread | 1/2 | cup maple sugar |
| 1/2 | cup butter, melted | 4 | tea. cinnamon |

Preheat electric frypan to 360°. Trim crusts from bread, cut in half; brush with butter; roll in sugar combined with cinnamon. Place in the ungreased pan; turn often until browned and serve hot.

## Sour Milk Bread

| | | | |
|---|---|---|---|
| 1 | egg, beaten | 2 | cups flour |
| 3/4 | cup maple sugar | 1 | tea. salt |
| 1 | cup sour milk with 1 tea. baking | 1/2 | tea. cinnamon |
| | soda dissolved in it | 1/2 | cup chopped nuts |

*Preheat oven to 350°. Cream the egg with the maple sugar; add sour milk mixture and blend well. Sift together the flour, salt and cinnamon and add to mixture. Fold in nuts. Place in greased loaf pan and bake one hour, or until done. Cool.*

## Tropical Pineapple Bread

| | | | |
|---|---|---|---|
| 1 | lb. 4 oz. crushed pineapple | 1/3 | cup finely chopped dates |
| 2 | cups flour | 3/4 | cup chopped walnuts |
| 1/2 | cup maple sugar | 1 | egg, beaten |
| 3 | tea. baking powder | 1/4 | cup melted butter |
| 1 | tea. salt | 1 1/2 | tea. vanilla extract |
| 1/2 | tea. baking soda | | |

*Preheat oven to 350°. Drain pineapple well. Sift flour, sugar, baking powder, salt, and baking soda into a large bowl. Add dates and walnuts; mix well. Add egg, pineapple, butter, and vanilla; with wooden spoon, stir just until well blended. Turn into a greased 9"x5"x3" loaf pan. Bake 1 hour, or until done. Cool for 15 minutes; remove from pan; cool completely. Serve with softened cream cheese if you desire.*

## Maple Bran Bread

1 1/2 cups flour
3     tea. baking powder
1     tea. salt
1/4   cup sugar
1 1/2 cups bran

1     egg, beaten
3/4   cup milk
1/2   cup maple syrup
4     Tbs. melted shortening

Preheat oven to 350°. Sift flour, baking powder, salt and sugar into a large bowl. Add remaining ingredients and mix well. Pour into a greased bread pan and bake 50 minutes, or until done; cool.

## Maple Graham Bread

3     cups graham flour
1     cup white flour
1     tea. salt
1     heaping tea. baking soda

1     cup milk
1     cup sour milk
1     cup maple syrup
1     cup chopped nuts

Preheat oven to 350°. In a large bowl combine all the ingredients and mix well. Place in two well greased loaf pans and bake for 50 minutes, or until done; cool.

### Maple Date and Nut Bread

| | | | | |
|---|---|---|---|---|
| 1 | cup shredded dates | | 1 | tea. salt |
| 3/4 | tea. baking soda | | 1 | cup flour |
| 1 | cup boiling water | | 1 | cup whole wheat flour |
| 1 | egg, beaten | | 1 | tea. baking powder |
| 1/2 | cup maple syrup | | 1/2 | cup chopped nuts |

Preheat oven to 350°. Mix together the dates, baking soda and boiling water. Add the egg and syrup and mix well. Beat in remaining ingredients. Pour into a greased bread pan and bake for one hour, or until done; cool.

### Maple Nut Brown Bread

| | | | | |
|---|---|---|---|---|
| 2 | cups flour | | 4 | Tbs. maple syrup |
| 4 | tea. baking powder | | 1 | egg, beaten |
| 1 | tea. salt | | 1 | cup chopped nuts _or_ raisins |
| 3/4 | cup milk | | | |

Preheat oven to 350°. Sift flour, baking powder and salt together. Add milk, syrup and beaten egg. Mix well. Add nuts _or_ raisins. Pour into a greased bread pan and bake for one hour, or until done; cool.

## Oatmeal Bread*

| | | | |
|---|---|---|---|
| 1 1/2 | cups boiling water | 2 | cups flour |
| 1 | cup oatmeal | 2 | tea. soft butter |
| 1/2 | cup warm water | 2 | tea. salt |
| 1 | tea. sugar | 4 | Tbs. maple syrup |
| 1/4 | tea. ginger | 2 | cups flour |
| 2 | pkgs. yeast | 1 | cup flour (for kneading) |
| 4 | Tbs. brown sugar | | |

Pour the boiling water over the oatmeal in a large bowl and let stand until warm. Combine the 1/2 cup warm water, sugar, ginger and yeast and let stand until bubbly. Add brown sugar and 2 cups of flour to the oatmeal mixture. Stir well and add yeast mixture, beating well. Add butter, salt, maple syrup and 2 cups of flour. Stir well.

Put remaining 1 cup of flour on a board and knead dough until stiff. Cover and let rise in a greased bowl until doubled in bulk. Turn out, knead well, and shape into two loaves. Put in bread pans, covered, and let rise until doubled in size. Bake in a 375° oven for 20 minutes, or until done. Cool before removing from pans. Yields 2 loaves, but recipe may be doubled for 4 loaves.

## Steamed Indian Bread

| | | | |
|---|---|---|---|
| 1 1/2 | cups wheat flour | 1 | tea. salt |
| 1 | cup corn meal | 1/2 | cup maple syrup |
| 1/2 | Tbs. baking soda | 1 2/3 | cup milk |

Sift together flour, corn meal, baking soda and salt. Add syrup and milk and mix well. Grease upper part of a double boiler and fill half full of batter. (Boiling water in lower half should cover 1/2" of base filled with bread batter.) Cover tightly and steam 3 hours over low heat, keeping water boiling gently. Add more boiling water as needed. Cool slightly before unmolding. Serve warm. Drizzle with maple syrup if you desire.

## Quick Nut Bread

| | | | |
|---|---|---|---|
| 2 | cups flour | 2 | Tbs. soft butter |
| 1/2 | cup maple sugar | 1 | egg |
| 2 | tea. baking powder | 1 | cup milk |
| 1 | tea. salt | 3/4 | cup chopped nuts |

Preheat oven to 350°. Sift first four ingredients together. Beat butter, egg and milk until smooth and add to the sifted ingredients, mixing well. Fold in nuts. Place in a greased bread pan and bake for 40 minutes, or until done; cool.

# Cookies

*"Oh, weary mothers mixing dough,*
*Don't you wish that cookies would grow?*
*Your lips would smile I know to see*
*A cookie bush or a candy tree!"*

*The Home Recipe Book, 1910*

## Chocolate Chip Cookies

| | | | | |
|---|---|---|---|---|
| 1/2 | cup butter, soft | | 1/2 | tea. baking soda |
| 1/4 | cup white sugar | | 1 1/8 | cups flour |
| 1/2 | cup maple sugar | | 1/2 | cup chopped nuts |
| 1 | egg, beaten | | 1 | tea. vanilla |
| 1/2 | tea. salt | | 7 | ozs. chocolate chips |

Preheat oven to 350°. Cream butter and both sugars together. Add all other ingredients, except chocolate chips, and mix well. Fold in chocolate chips. Drop by spoonfull onto greased cookie sheet. Bake for 15 minutes, or until done. Yields about 2 dozen cookies.

## Gumdrop Cookies

| | | | | |
|---|---|---|---|---|
| 4 | eggs | | 1/4 | tea. salt |
| 1 | Tbs. cold water | | 1 | tea. cinnamon |
| 2 | cups maple sugar | | 1/2 | cup chopped nuts |
| 2 | cups flour | | 1 | cup small gumdrops, cut in half |

Preheat oven to 325°. Beat eggs well with cold water. Add sugar slowly and beat until fluffy. Stir together flour, salt and cinnamon and beat into sugar mixture. Add nuts and gumdrops and fold into mixture. Drop by spoonfulls onto greased cookie sheet and bake 15 minutes, or until done. Yields about 2 1/2 dozen cookies.

## Nut Spice Cookies

| | | | | |
|---|---|---|---|---|
| 1 | cup shortening | 1/2 | tea. salt |
| 1/2 | cup white sugar | 2 | tea. cinnamon |
| 1/2 | cup maple sugar | 1/4 | tea. nutmeg |
| 1 | egg | 1/4 | tea. cloves |
| 2 1/4 | cups sifted flour | 1/2 | cup chopped nuts |
| 1/2 | tea. baking soda | | |

Preheat oven to 350°. Cream shortening and sugars. Add egg and beat well. Sift together flour, baking soda, salt and spices. Stir into the creamed mixture. Stir in nuts. Shape into two rolls, wrap in waxed paper, and chill for an hour. Slice very thin and bake for 5 minutes, or until done. Yields 3 dozen cookies.

## Chocolate Drops

| | | | | |
|---|---|---|---|---|
| 1 1/4 | cups sifted flour | 1 | tea. vanilla |
| 1/4 | tea. baking soda | 1/2 | tea. salt |
| 1 | cup soft shortening | 1/2 | cup buttermilk |
| 1 | cup maple sugar, packed | 1 | cup walnuts, |
| 1 | egg | | coarsely chopped |
| 2 | sq. unsweetened chocolate, melted | | |

Preheat oven to 350°. Sift flour with baking soda. Mix shortening, maple sugar, egg, chocolate, vanilla and salt until well blended. Stir in flour mixture, then buttermilk. Stir in nuts. Onto greased cookie sheets, drop level tablespoons of dough, 2" apart. Bake 12 minutes, or until top springs back when lightly touched. Cool before serving. Yields 2 dozen cookies.

## Old English Dropped Cookies

| | | | |
|---|---|---|---|
| 1 | cup shortening | 1 | tea. baking soda |
| 2 | eggs, beaten | 1 | tea. cinnamon |
| 2 | cups maple sugar | 1 | tea. nutmeg |
| 1 | cup cold black coffee | 2 | cups raisins |
| 3 | cups flour | 1 | cup chopped nuts |
| 1 | tea. baking powder | | |

Preheat oven to 375°. In a large bowl use electric mixer to beat first 4 ingredients until smooth. Sift together the flour, baking powder, baking soda and spices. Add to first mixture and beat until smooth. Fold in raisins and nuts. Drop by spoonfuls on greased cookie sheet and bake for 10 minutes, or until done. Yields about 3 dozen cookies.

## Quick Sugar Cookies

| | | | |
|---|---|---|---|
| 1 | cup butter, soft | 2 | cups flour |
| 1/2 | cup maple sugar | 1/4 | tea. baking powder |
| | | 1/4 | tea. salt |

Preheat oven to 350°. Cream together butter and maple sugar. Sift together flour, baking powder and salt; add to creamed mixture and mix well. Roll out to 1/4" thickness on a floured board and cut with floured cookie cutter. Prick with a fork. Bake 20 minutes, or until done. Yields about 2 dozen cookies.

## Maple-Lemon Cookies

| | | | | |
|---|---|---|---|---|
| 1 | cup shortening | | 2 | Tbs. milk |
| 2 | cups maple sugar | | 5 | cups flour |
| 4 | eggs, beaten | | 1/2 | tea. salt |
| 1 | tea. lemon extract | | 2 | tea. baking powder |

Preheat oven to 350°. Cream shortening and maple sugar together. Add eggs, lemon extract and milk and mix well. Sift together flour, salt and baking powder and add to mixture, beat well. Drop by spoonfuls onto greased cookie sheet and flatten with a fork. Sprinkle with maple sugar if you desire. Bake for 10 minutes, or until done. Yields about 4 dozen cookies.

## Fruit Ice-Box Cookies

| | | | | |
|---|---|---|---|---|
| 2 | cups maple sugar | | 1/2 | tea. salt |
| 3 1/2 | cups flour | | 1 | tea. baking soda, scant |
| 1 | cup melted butter | | 1/2 | cup candied cherries |
| 1/2 | tea. baking powder | | 1/2 | cup chopped nuts |
| 1 | tea. vanilla | | 1/2 | cup raisins |
| 2 | eggs, beaten | | | |

Preheat oven to 375°. In a large bowl mix first 8 ingredients together with electric mixer on medium speed for 3 minutes. Fold in cherries, nuts and raisins. Shape into rolls, wrap in waxed paper and chill for 1 hour. Slice and bake on greased cookie sheet for 10 minutes, or until done. Yields about 3 dozen cookies.

## Maple Dropped Cookies

| | | | |
|---|---|---|---|
| 1 | beaten egg | 1 1/4 | cups flour |
| 1/2 | cup soft butter | 1/2 | tea. baking soda |
| 1/2 | cup maple syrup | 1/2 | tea. salt |
| 1/2 | cup chopped nuts | | |

Preheat oven to 325°. In a large bowl stir together egg, butter and syrup. Stir in nuts. Sift together flour, baking soda and salt and add to mixture. Drop by spoonfuls onto greased cookie sheet. Bake for 8 minutes, or until done. Yields about 2 dozen cookies.

## Sour Cream Oatmeal Cookies

| | | | |
|---|---|---|---|
| 1 | cup shortening | 1 | tea. cinnamon |
| 1 | cup sugar | 1 | tea. ginger |
| 1/4 | cup maple syrup | 1/2 | cup sour cream |
| 2 | cups flour | 3 | cups quick-cooking oatmeal |
| 1 | tea. salt | | |

Preheat oven to 375°. Cream shortening and sugar together. Add maple syrup and flour and mix well. Add remaining ingredients and stir until smooth and well mixed. Drop spoonfuls of batter onto greased cookie sheet and bake for 12 minutes, or until done. Yields about 3 dozen cookies.

## Maple Refrigerator Cookies

| | | | | |
|---|---|---|---|---|
| 3 | cups flour | | 1 | cup butter, softened |
| 1/2 | tea. baking soda | | 1 | cup maple sugar |
| 1/4 | tea. salt | | 1 | tea. vanilla |
| 1 | egg, beaten | | 1/2 | cup chopped nuts |

Preheat oven to 350º. In a large bowl sift together flour, baking soda and salt. Add egg, butter, sugar and vanilla and mix together well. Stir in nuts. Shape into a roll and chill dough for one hour. Slice and bake for 12 minutes, or until done. Yields 2 1/2 dozen cookies.

## Ginger Snaps

| | | | | |
|---|---|---|---|---|
| 1/2 | cup shortening | | 1/2 | cup sour cream |
| 1 | cup maple sugar | | 1/2 | tea. baking soda |
| 1 | egg, beaten | | 1 | tea. ginger |
| | | | 1-2 | cups flour |

Preheat oven to 450º. Cream together shortening and maple sugar. Add beaten egg. Mix together sour cream, baking soda and ginger and add to first mixture. Mix well. Add enough flour to make a workable dough (1/2 cup at a time) and blend thoroughly. Roll out on a floured board to 1/4" thickness and cut with floured cookie cutter. Put on greased cookie sheet and bake 8 minutes or until done. Yields about 2 1/2 dozen cookies.

## Soft Maple Ginger Cookies

| | | | | |
|---|---|---|---|---|
| 1 | cup sugar | 1 | tea. cinnamon |
| 1/2 | cup softened butter | 1 | tea. ginger |
| 1/2 | cup lard | 1/4 | tea. _each_ cloves, allspice, nutmeg |
| 1 | egg | | |
| 1 | cup maple syrup | 1 | tea. salt |
| 1 | cup sour milk | 5 | cups flour (about) |
| 2 | tea. baking soda | | |

Preheat oven to 375°. Cream sugar, butter and lard together. Add egg and mix well. Stir in maple syrup and milk. Add all remaining ingredients except flour and beat well. Add 4 to 5 cups of flour, making a dough stiff enough to roll. Chill thoroughly (1-2 hours). Roll dough out on floured board to 1/4" thick and cut with cookie cutter. Bake on a greased cookie sheet about 12 minutes, or until done. Yields about 6 dozen cookies.

## Maple Wafer Cookies

| | | | | |
|---|---|---|---|---|
| 1/2 | cup maple syrup | 1 | cup flour |
| 1/2 | cup sugar | 1/2 | tea. baking powder |
| 1/2 | cup butter | 1/4 | tea. baking soda |

Preheat oven to 350°. Slowly heat syrup, sugar and butter to boiling point. Boil one minute and remove from fire. Sift flour, baking powder and baking soda together and add to syrup mixture. Stir well. Set pan in a vessel of hot water to keep from hardening. On a buttered cookie sheet drop teaspoons of batter 3" apart and bake for 10 minutes, or until done. Cool slightly and lift carefully with a thin knife. Yields 4 to 5 dozen cookies.

## Cornflake Cookies

1/2 cup shortening
3/4 cup maple sugar
1 egg, beaten
3 Tbs. milk
1 tea. vanilla

1 1/4 cups flour
1/2 tea. baking soda
1 1/4 cups cornflakes
1/2 cup chopped raisins

Preheat oven to 350°. Cream shortening, sugar and egg. Add milk and vanilla and mix well. Sift together flour and baking soda and add to first mixture. Stir in cornflakes and raisins. Drop from teaspoon on greased cookie sheet and bake 12 minutes, or until done. Yields about 2 dozen cookies.

## Maple Nut Cookies

3 cups flour
1 tea. baking powder
1/2 tea. salt
1 1/2 cups maple sugar
3 eggs, beaten

1 tea. baking soda
1/2 cup hot water
1 cup chopped nuts
1 1/2 cup raisins (optional)

Preheat oven to 375°. Sift together flour, baking powder and salt. Add maple sugar and eggs and beat well. Dissolve baking soda in the hot water and add to mixture; mix well. Fold in nuts and raisins. Drop by spoonfuls onto a greased cookie sheet and bake 10 minutes, or until done. Yields about 3 dozen cookies.

## Peanut Butter Cookies

| | | | |
|---|---|---|---|
| 3 | Tbs. shortening | 1 1/2 | cups flour |
| 1 | cup maple sugar | 1 | tea. baking soda |
| 1 | egg, beaten | 1/2 | tea. salt |
| 3 | Tbs. sour cream | 1/2 | cup peanut butter |

Preheat oven to 450°. Cream shortening with maple sugar. Add egg and sour cream. Sift flour, baking soda and salt together. Add to first mixture and stir well. Add peanut butter and beat until smooth. Drop tablespoons of batter onto greased cookie sheet and criss-cross with f fork to flatten. Bake 10 minutes, or until done. Yields about 2 dozen cookies.

1992344

## Maple Sugar Cookies

| | | | |
|---|---|---|---|
| 1/2 | cup shortening | 1 | egg, beaten |
| 1 1/2 | cups maple sugar | 1/2 | tea. baking soda |
| 1 | tea. salt | 1/2 | cup milk |
| | | 3 | cups flour |

Preheat oven to 425°. Cream together the shortening, maple sugar and salt. Add egg and mix well. Add baking soda, milk and flour and beat until smooth. Roll out to 1/4" thickness on a floured board and cut with floured cookie cutter. Bake for 10 minutes, or until done. Yields about 3 dozen cookies.

## Maple Oatmeal Dropped Cookies

| | | | |
|---|---|---|---|
| 1/2 | cup shortening | 2 | tea. baking soda |
| 1 | cup maple syrup | 1/4 | cup milk |
| 1 | egg, beaten | 1 1/2 | cups oatmeal |
| 1 1/2 | cups flour | 1/2 | cup raisins |
| 1 | tea. salt | 1/2 | cup chopped nuts |

Preheat oven to 375⁰. Beat shortening, maple syrup and egg together until fluffy. Sift flour, salt and baking soda together. Add to first mixture. Add milk and oatmeal and mix well. Stir in raisins and nuts. Drop by spoonfuls on a greased cookie sheet. Bake for 15 minutes, or until done. Yields about 3 dozen cookies.

## Maple Hermits*

| | | | |
|---|---|---|---|
| 1/2 | cup shortening | 1/2 | tea. salt |
| 1 1/4 | cups sugar | 1/4 | tea. cloves |
| 1 | egg (plus 1 egg, beaten) | 1 | tea. ginger |
| 1/4 | cup maple syrup | 1 | tea. cinnamon |
| 3 | cups flour | 2 1/2 | ozs. water |
| 1 1/2 | tea. baking soda | 1 | cup raisins |

Preheat oven to 350⁰. Cream shortening and sugar together. Mix in one egg and maple syrup. Sift together flour, baking soda, salt and spices. Add this mixture to the former one and mix well. Stir in water and raisins. Divide into three balls and roll between hands to form three sausage-like strips and place on greased cookie sheet. Brush with beaten egg and bake 15 minutes, or until done. Cool and cut into bars. Yields 15-20 bars.

## Holiday Coconut Nuggets

| | | | |
|---|---|---|---|
| 3/4 | cup butter | 1/2 | tea. salt |
| 3/4 | cup maple sugar, packed | 1 | cup flaked coconut |
| 1 | egg | 3/4 | cup raisins |
| 1 | tea. grated lemon rind | 1/4 | cup candied cherries, |
| 2 | cups sifted flour | | coarsely chopped |

Preheat oven to 350°. Cream butter until soft; add sugar gradually, creaming thoroughly until light and fluffy. Stir in egg and lemon rind. Sift flour and salt into creamed mixture; mix to form a stiff dough. Stir in coconut, raisins, and cherries. Drop by spoonfuls onto a greased cookie sheet. Bake 15 minutes, or until golden. Cool. Yields about 2 dozen cookies.

## Peanut Chunkies

| | | | |
|---|---|---|---|
| 1 1/3 | cups sifted flour | 1/3 | cup white sugar |
| 1/2 | tea. baking powder | 1/2 | cup maple sugar, packed |
| 3/4 | tea. baking soda | 1 | egg |
| 1/4 | tea. salt | 1 | cup <u>unsalted</u> peanuts, |
| 1/2 | cup soft butter | | chopped |
| 2/3 | cup cream-style peanut butter | | |

Preheat oven to 350°. Sift flour, baking powder, baking soda and salt together. Beat butter, peanut butter, sugars and egg in a bowl until light and fluffy; mix in sifted dry ingredients. Pinch off small pieces of dough, roll gently into cylinder shapes between palms of hands. Roll in chopped peantus to coat well. Place 2" apart on greased cookie sheet and press down slightly with a spatula. Bake 10 minutes or until done. Cool. Yields about 2 dozen cookies.

## Dipped Cinnamon Cookies

| | | | |
|---|---|---|---|
| 2 3/4 | cups sifted flour | 1 1/2 | cups white sugar |
| 2 | tea. cream of tartar | 2 | eggs |
| 1 | tea. baking soda | 1 | egg white, slightly beaten |
| 1/2 | tea. salt | 4 | Tbs. maple sugar |
| 1 | cup butter | 2 | Tbs. cinnamon |

Preheat oven to 350°. Sift flour, cream of tartar, baking soda and salt together. Beat butter, 1 1/2 cups white sugar, and eggs together in bowl until light and fluffy. Add dry ingredients, blend. Shape dough into small balls; dip in egg white then in mixture of maple sugar and cinnamon stirred together. Place on greased cookie sheet about 2" apart and press down centers with tines of fork. Bake 12 minutes, or until lightly browned. Cool. Yields about 3 dozen cookies.

## Birds' Nest Cookies

| | | | |
|---|---|---|---|
| 2 | cups sifted flour | 2 | egg yolks |
| 1/4 | tea. salt | 1 | tea. vanilla |
| 1 | cup soft butter | 2 | egg whites, slightly beaten |
| 1/2 | cup maple sugar, packed | 2 | cups chopped nuts |
| | | | Preserves or jellies |

Preheat oven to 350°. Sift flour and salt together. Beat butter, sugar, egg yolks, and vanilla in a bowl until light and fluffy. Stir in sifted ingredients; mix until smooth. Pinch off small pieces of dough; roll gently between palms of hands to form balls. Dip in egg white, then in chopped nuts; place about 2" apart on a greased cookie sheet. Flatten with palm of hand, make indentation in center of each with thumb. Bake 12 minutes, or until done. Cool. Fill centers of cooled cookies with your favorite preserves and/or jellies.

# Candies

*"My homemade maple sweets afford me much consolation to reflect that they possess no mingled tears of misery; no slave ever groaned over my caldrons or fanned them with his sighs. No, this little lump in my hand is the reward of my own labor on my own farm."*

*Farmer's Almanac, 1804*

## About Making Candies

Since a variety of cooks have submitted these candy recipes, there are tw[cut] methods shown to determine candy temperature—either by the ice water test c[cut] the candy thermometer reading. Printed below are the equivalent thermomete[cut] temperatures as related to the ice water method so that you may use either on[cut]

### When syrup is dropped into ice water it:

Threads off a spoon and looks like a coarse thread in water — $230^o$-$234$[cut]

Forms a soft ball and flattens when touched — $234^o$-$240^o$

Forms a firm ball that holds its shape even when touched — $242^o$-$248$[cut]

Forms a hard ball that will hold its shape but looks pliable — $250^o$-$268$[cut]

Will separate into hard threads and hold its shape — $270^o$-$290^o$ — calle[cut] soft crack

Will separate into threads that are hard and brittle when removed fror[cut] the water — $300^o$-$310^o$ — called hard crack

It's best to use a deep and heavy saucepan to boil candies, as foam wi[cut] sometimes rise quickly and high. Also, it is best to use a wooden spoon to kee[cut] your hands from burning; metal spoons can alter your candy's temperature, o[cut] even leave a metallic taste.

## Maple Sugar — Soft and Hard*

By simply boiling maple syrup you can make what is called maple sugar. oft sugar can be put into molds and served as candy or stored in airtight con- iners to use in any recipe calling for maple sugar. Hard sugar is best used only r candy making, but should you decide to use it in recipes it must be shaved or ated to measure correctly.

One pint of maple syrup will yield about one pound of either soft or hard igar; muffin tins filled up about 1/2" may be substituted for candy molds; easing is not necessary.

### For soft sugar or soft sugar candy:

Boil Fancy or Grade A syrup until it is $32^o$ above the boiling point of ater as registered by your candy thermometer. Remove from heat and cool to 75°. Stir slowly until gloss is lost and pour into candy molds. Cool to room mperature before serving. (Should you want the sugar for cooking purposes, mply cool the sugar to room temperature and put into airtight containers.)

### For hard sugar or hard sugar candy:

Boil Fancy or Grade A maple syrup until it is $38^o$ above the boiling point f water as registered by your candy thermometer. Remove from heat and cool 175°. Stir slowly until gloss is lost and pour into molds. Cool to room mperature before serving. (For hard sugar to be used in recipes, simply store igar in airtight containers and grate to measure when needed.)

Note: In making the above sugars a certain amount of foam always develops; bring it back down drop in a teaspoon of butter.

## Maple Divinity Fudge*

| | | | |
|---|---|---|---|
| 2 | cups sugar | 1/2 | cup cherries |
| 2 | cups maple syrup, Fancy or Grade A | 1/2 | cup raisins |
| 2 | egg whites, stiffly beaten | 1 | cup chopped nuts |

Boil sugar and syrup to 260° on candy thermometer. Pour mixtue slowl, over beaten egg whites and beat until thick. Add cherries, raisins, and nuts. Turi into 12" square pan to cool. Yields 12-16 pieces.

## Maple Caramels

| | | | |
|---|---|---|---|
| 1/3 | cup brown sugar | 1 | Tbs. butter |
| 1/3 | cup white sugar | 1/4 | tea. salt |
| 3/4 | cup maple syrup, Fancy or Grade A | 1/2 | cup chopped nuts |
| 1/2 | cup light cream | 1 | tea. vanilla |

Cook both sugars, syrup and cream together until it forms a hard ball whei dropped in cold water. Add remaining ingredients and stir <u>once.</u> Withou beating, pour into buttered 8" pan and chill. Cut into squares. Store in waxe paper. Yields 12-16 squares.

## Pecan Candy

| | | | |
|---|---|---|---|
| 4 | cups molasses | 1/2 | tea. cider vinegar |
| 1 | cup brown sugar | pinch | of salt |
| 1 | cup maple sugar | 1 | tea. vanilla extract |
| pinch | cream of tartar | 1/2 | tea. almond extract |
| 1/2 | cup soft butter | 2 | cups chopped pecans |

Cook the molasses, sugars and cream of tartar to 256° on candy thermometer. Add the butter, vinegar, salt, extracts and pecans. Stir lightly to blend and pour into a 9" buttered pan; cool to room temperature before cutting. Yields 12-16 pieces of candy.

## Quick Maple Fudge

| | | | |
|---|---|---|---|
| 2 | cups white sugar | 1 | Tbs. corn syrup |
| 1 | cup maple syrup, Fancy or Grade A | 1 | cup milk |

Put all ingredients into a saucepan and cook to 236° on candy thermometer. Cool slightly and beat until creamy. Pour into a buttered 8" square pan and cool to room temperature before cutting. Yields 12-16 squares of fudge.

## Peanut Butter Fudge

| | | | | |
|---|---|---|---|---|
| 2 | cups maple sugar | | 1/2 | tea. salt |
| 3/4 | cup milk | | 2 | Tbs. soft peanut butter |
| 1/4 | cup light cream | | | |

Put sugar, milk, cream and salt into a saucepan and cook until 236° on candy thermometer. Remove from heat, add peanut butter and beat until creamy. Pour into a buttered 8" square pan and cool to room temperature before cutting. Yields 12-16 squares of fudge.

## Maple Nut Balls

| | | | | |
|---|---|---|---|---|
| 1 | tea. butter, soft | | 1 | cup heavy cream |
| 2 | cups maple sugar | | 1/2 | tea. cream of tartar |
| 1 | cup white sugar | | 1 | cup walnuts, pulverized |

Spread the butter evenly over the sides of an 8"x6" baking dish.

Combine the sugars, heavy cream and cream of tartar in a heavy 4 quart saucepan. Boil _slowly_ until temperature reaches 240° on candy thermometer. (Do not stir or cover.) Pour the candy into the buttered dish; cool to room temperature and chill for 3 hours. Put the candy mixture into a deep bowl and beat until creamy. Roll small pieces of candy into balls and roll gently in the walnuts. Refrigerate until ready to serve. Makes 2-3 dozen balls.

## Maple Pralines

| | | | |
|---|---|---|---|
| 2 | cups sugar | 1 | cup maple syrup, Fancy or Grade A |
| 2/3 | cup milk | 1 1/2 | cups chopped pecans |

Boil sugar, milk and syrup until it forms a soft ball when dropped in cold water. Remove from heat and cool to luke-warm. Beat until creamy, add pecans, and drop from tip of spoon in small mounds on buttered waxed paper. Yields 2 dozen candies.

## Maple Brittle

| | | | |
|---|---|---|---|
| 3 | cups maple sugar | 2 | tea. baking soda |
| 1 | cup cold water | 1 | Tbs. boiling water |
| 1 | cup maple syrup, plus 1 Tbs. | 1 | tea. lemon extract |
| pinch | cream of tartar | 1 | cup chopped nuts of your choice |
| 1/2 | cup soft butter | | |

Cook the sugar, water, maple syrup and cream of tartar to 300° on a candy thermometer. Add the butter, boil for 4 minutes; remove from heat. Dissolve baking soda in the boiling water and add to mixture. Add lemon extract. Wait until mixture starts to foam and pour out onto greased cookie sheets, spreading very thin. Sprinkle with nuts and cool to room temperature. Break into pieces and serve.

## Maple Puffed Rice Candy

1      cup maple syrup, Fancy or Grade A      1 1/2   cups   puffed   rice,   slightly oven-warmed   to   make   crisp

1      Tbs. butter

Boil syrup until soft ball stage. Remove from heat, add butter and beat until it begins to thicken. Add puffed rice and mix thoroughly. Drop by table-spoons full onto waxed paper and cool to room temperature. Yields 1 1/2 dozen candies.

## Maple Sugar Fudge

2      cups white sugar              1      Tbs. butter
1      cup maple sugar              1      tea. vanilla
2/3   cup milk                      1      cup chopped nuts

Cook both sugars and milk to the boiling point and boil slowly for 12 minutes. Remove from heat and add butter and vanilla. Cool slightly, then beat until thick and creamy. Fold in nuts and pour into an 8" buttered pan. Cool and cut into squares. Yields 9 — 12 pieces of fudge.

## Maple Popcorn Balls

1 1/2 quarts cooked popcorn

1/2    tea. salt
1    tea. butter

1/2    cup maple syrup, Fancy or
      Grade A
1/4    cup sugar

Sprinkle salt over popped corn. Cook butter, syrup and sugar to 275°
on candy thermometer. Pour over popcorn, stirring constantly. Dip hands in
cold water and shape popcorn balls. Yields 9 — 12 balls.

## Maple Syrup Fudge

1    cup maple syrup, Fancy or Grade A

1    cup sugar
1/2    cup milk

Mix syrup, sugar and milk in a large saucepan and cook slowly to 235°-
240° on a candy thermometer. Stir frequently. Remove from heat and cool to
120°. Beat until creamy and fudge has lost its gloss. Pour into greased 8" square
pan and cut when cool. Yields 12 1" squares.

## Maple Creams

| | | | |
|---|---|---|---|
| 1 | cup maple sugar | 1/2 | tea. almond extract |
| 1 | cup light brown sugar | 24 | walnut halves |
| 1/4 | cup water | | |

Cook sugars and water to 240°. Add the almond extract. Cool to room temperature and beat until creamy, yet firm. Knead the candy until smooth; form into small balls and press a walnut half into each ball. Yields 2 dozen creams.

## Chocolate Maple Fudge

| | | | |
|---|---|---|---|
| 1 | cup maple sugar | 2 | squares chocolate, shaved |
| 1 | cup brown sugar | 3/4 | cup light cream |
| 2 | Tbs. butter | 1/2 | cup nuts, chopped |
| 3/4 | cup maple syrup, Fancy or Grade A | | |

Place the sugars, butter, syrup, chocolate and cream in a saucepan and cook, stirring constantly, to 240°. Remove from heat and beat until creamy. Pour into a 9" square buttered pan; sprinkle with nuts and cool to room temperature before cutting. Yields 12 pieces of fudge.

# Puddings

*And if the dish contentment brings,
you'll dine with me again.*

The Home Recipe Book, 1910

## Maple Bread Pudding*

| 7 | slices of bread | 2/3 | cup maple syrup |
|---|---|---|---|
| 1 | tea. cinnamon | 2 | eggs, beaten |
| 3 | cups scalded milk | 1 | tea. salt |

Preheat oven to 350°. Break bread into pieces and put into a buttered 2-quart baking dish; sprinkle cinnamon over bread. Pour scalded milk over bread. Mix remaining ingredients together and stir into bread crumbs. Bake for 1 hour, or until done. Serves 5.

## Baked Maple Pudding

| 1 | Tbs. soft butter | 3 | egg yolks, beaten |
|---|---|---|---|
| 1/2 | cup maple sugar | 2/3 | cup evaporated milk |
| 1/2 | cup maple syrup | 1/3 | cup cold water |
| 2 | Tbs. flour | 1 | Tbs. melted butter, cooled |
| 1 | tea. lemon juice | 3 | egg whites |
| 1/2 | tea. vanilla | pinch of salt | |

Preheat oven to 350°. Spread the soft butter evenly over the bottom and sides of a 2-quart baking dish. Combine the maple sugar, syrup, flour, lemon juice, vanilla and salt in a deep bowl and mix well. Beat in the egg yolks; add evaporated milk, water and butter and stir until mixture is smooth. Beat egg whites until stiff and fold them into the maple sugar mixture gently and thoroughly. Pour into the buttered dish and set in a large shallow roasting pan. Place the pan in the middle of the oven and pour enough boiling water in to reach halfway up the sides of the dish. Bake for 45 minutes, or until top is golden brown. Serve warm. Serves 6.

## Maple Cottage Pudding

*Note: Although this recipe is called a "pudding," it is actually an old recipe that adds flour to turn it into a cake that is served thinly sliced. We have included it so that some of our grandmother friends may enjoy the recipe again and the younger people may see what they've been missing!*

| | | | | |
|---|---|---|---|---|
| 1/2 | cup maple syrup | | 1/2 | cup milk |
| 1 | Tbs. shortening | | 1 | cup flour |
| 3 | Tbs. sugar | | 2 | tea. baking powder |
| 1 | egg | | 1/2 | cup chopped nuts |
| 1/2 | tea. salt | | | |

Preheat oven to 400°. Bring syrup to the boiling point and pour into bottom of a loaf pan. With an electric mixer beat all the remaining ingredients until smooth. Pour this thick batter slowly over syrup, covering all the syrup. Bake for 25 minutes, or until done. After removing from oven, carefully turn the cake upside down on a large platter. Slice and <u>serve  warm</u>.

## Banana Pudding

| | | | | |
|---|---|---|---|---|
| 5 | fresh sliced bananas | | 2 | Tbs. light cream |
| 1 | cup maple syrup | | 3 | Tbs. butter |
| | | | | whipped cream, optional |

Over low heat in a saucepan mix syrup, cream and butter and cook slowly for 10 minutes. Pour, while hot, over bananas and serve at once. Top with whipped cream if desired. Serves 4.

*Note: Depending on how hot your stove runs, the syrup may be too hot to pour immediately over bananas. Cool and stir for 10 minutes or so until you feel it is not too hot.*

## Indian Pudding*

3 1/2 cups milk, scalded
1/2 cup corn meal
1 tea. cinnamon
1/4 tea. cloves
1 tea. salt

1/4 tea. ginger
1 egg, beaten
2/3 cup maple syrup
1/2 cup milk (for topping)

Preheat oven to 275°. Scald milk. Meanwhile sift together the corn meal, cinnamon, cloves, salt and ginger. Add egg and maple syrup to scalded milk and mix well. To this mixture add the sifted ingredients and stir well. Pour into greased baking dish (2-3 quart). Pour the 1/2 cup milk over top slowly. Bake for 2 hours, or until firm. Serves 4-6.

## Steamed Maple Pudding

1 cup maple syrup
1 cup milk
1 cup raisins
1/2 cup melted butter
1/2 tea. salt

1/2 tea. cinnamon
1/4 tea. nutmeg _and_ cloves
1 tea. baking soda
4 cups flour

In a large bowl with your electric mixer set on medium speed mix all ingredients, except raisins, until well blended. Fold in raisins. Grease two 1-pound coffee cans and pour batter into each one to fill only half-way. Cover with aluminum foil; set containers in a pot filled with water half-way up the coffee cans. Bring the water to a gentle boil and steam 3 hours, or until pudding is firm. Serves 8-10.

## Apple-Rice Pudding

| | | | |
|---|---|---|---|
| | cups cooked rice | 3 | Tbs. maple syrup |
| | apples, peeled and sliced thinly | 2 | Tbs. light brown sugar |

Preheat oven to 350°. Combine rice with brown sugar and maple syrup. Add the apples and stir lightly to mix. Place in a buttered 1 1/2 quart casserole; cover and bake for 30 minutes, or until apples are tender. Serve warm, with whipped cream, if desired. Serves 4.

## Maple Walnut Tapioca*

| | | | |
|---|---|---|---|
| | pint milk | 1 | egg yolk, beaten |
| /4 | cup tapioca | 1/2 | cup chopped walnuts |
| /3 | cup maple syrup | 1 | stiffly beaten egg white |
| /2 | tea. salt | | |

In a double boiler scald milk, tapioca, syrup and salt. Cook slowly for 15 minutes, stirring frequently. Take out a few spoonfuls to cool; add them to the egg yolk. Combine mixtures and stir well. Remove from heat and stir for 3 minutes. Cool to room temperature. Add walnuts and fold in egg white. May be served at once or chilled. Serves 6.

## Rhubarb Upside-Down Pudding

| | | | |
|---|---|---|---|
| 2 | cups diced rhubarb | 1/2 | tea. salt |
| 1 | Tbs. flour | 1/4 | cup shortening |
| 2/3 | cup maple syrup | 1 | egg, beaten |
| 1 | tea. grated orange rind | 3 | Tbs. each, milk and orange |
| 1 | tea. cinnamon | | juice |
| 1 | cup flour | 2 | Tbs. maple syrup |
| 2 | tea. baking powder | | |

Preheat oven to 350º. Mix rhubarb, 1 Tbs. flour, maple syrup, orange rind and cinnamon together and put in well greased 8" square pan. Sift together the 1 cup of flour, salt and baking powder. Cut in shortening. Mix together the egg, milk and orange juice. Add it to the shortening mixture and stir only until moistened. Spread on rhubarb and bake 25 minutes. Drizzle 2 Tbs. of maple syrup over top and bake 15 minutes longer, or until done. Turn out and serve warm. Serves 6.

## Maple Custard

| | | | |
|---|---|---|---|
| 1 | cup maple syrup | 1/4 | tea. salt |
| 2 | eggs, beaten | 1 | cup scalded milk |

Preheat oven to 325º. Mix syrup, eggs and salt together well. Add scalded milk very slowly to syrup solution, stirring constantly. Pour into 4 custard cups and place in a pan containing 1/2" of water. Bake for one hour, or until firm.

# Cakes and Icings

*"Let's put the cake in the oven to grow, ma."*
*Jennifer Lewis, age 4*
*1976*

## Spice Pound Cake

| | | | |
|---|---|---|---|
| 2/3 | cup soft butter | 1 | tea. cinnamon |
| 3/4 | cup sugar | 1/2 | tea. allspice |
| 2 | eggs, beaten | 1/4 | tea. cloves |
| 2/3 | cup milk | 1/4 | tea. mace |
| 2/3 | cup maple syrup | 1/2 | cup raisins, floured |
| 2 | cups flour | 1/3 | cup citron, cut up in |
| 3/4 | tea. baking soda | | strips, floured |

Preheat oven to 350°. Cream butter and sugar; add eggs, milk and syrup and mix well. Sift flour with baking soda and spices. Add to syrup mixture; beat well. Fold in raisins and citron. Bake in a large buttered cake pan for 30 minutes, or until done.

## Rhubarb Cake

| | | | |
|---|---|---|---|
| 2 | cups flour | 1 | cup milk |
| 1 | tea. baking soda | 1 | tea. vanilla |
| 1/4 | tea. salt | 2 1/2 | cups rhubarb in 1" pieces, |
| 1 1/2 | cups maple sugar | | thawed if frozen |
| 1/2 | cup butter | 1/2 | cup white sugar mixed with |
| 1 | egg, beaten | | 1 tea. cinnamon |

Preheat oven to 350°. Sift together flour, baking soda and salt. Set aside. In a large bowl beat maple sugar and butter together until well blended. Add egg. Beat in flour mixture alternately with milk until well blended. Stir in vanilla and rhubarb. Turn into a greased 9"x13" pan and sprinkle with sugar-cinnamon mixture. Bake for 35 minutes, or until done. Cool cake before turning out. Serves 8.

## Chocolate Fudge Cake

| | | | | |
|---|---|---|---|---|
| 2 | cups flour | | 1 1/4 | cups maple sugar |
| 1 1/2 | tea. baking powder | | 1 | tea. vanilla |
| 1/2 | tea. baking soda | | 2 | eggs, beaten |
| 1/2 | tea. salt | | 3 | squares chocolate, melted |
| 1/2 | cup butter, soft | | 1 | cup milk |

Preheat oven to 350°. Sift together flour, baking powder, baking soda and salt. With an electric mixer beat butter and maple sugar until fluffy. Add vanilla, eggs and chocolate and blend well. Add flour mixture alternately with milk until you have a smooth batter. Bake in 2 greased 8" cake pans for 25 minutes or until done.

## Crunchy Coconut Cake

| | | | | |
|---|---|---|---|---|
| 1 | cup flour | | 1/2 | cup shredded coconut |
| 1 | tea. baking powder | | 1/3 | cup shortening |
| 1/2 | tea. salt | | 3/4 | cup maple sugar |
| 1/2 | cup oatmeal | | 2 | eggs, beaten |
| 1/2 | cup chopped nuts | | 1/2 | tea. vanilla |

Preheat oven to 350°. Sift together flour, baking powder and salt. Stir in oatmeal, nuts and coconut. Cream together shortening and sugar; beat in eggs and vanilla. Stir in flour mixture. Spread in a buttered 9" square pan and bake for 25 minutes, or until done. Cut while warm and serve at once. Yields 12 squares.

## Maple Sugar Cake

| | | | | |
|---|---|---|---|---|
| 1/2 | cup shortening | | 2 | cups flour |
| 1 1/2 | cups maple sugar | | 2 | tea. baking powder |
| 2 | eggs, beaten | | 1/2 | tea. salt |
| | | | 1 | cup milk |

Preheat oven to 350°. Cream together the shortening and maple sugar. Beat in the eggs. Sift together the flour, bak9ng powder and salt and add to the mixture alternately with milk. Mix well. Bake in a 9" pan for 30 minutes, or until done.

## Maple Date Cake

| | | | | |
|---|---|---|---|---|
| 1 1/2 | cups maple sugar | | 3 | tea. baking powder |
| 1 | cup butter, soft | | 1/2 | tea. cinnamon |
| 2 | eggs, beaten | | 1/2 | tea. nutmeg |
| 1/2 | cup milk | | 1/2 | lb. dates, chopped |
| 1 3/4 | cup flour | | (1/2 | cup flour for dates) |

Preheat oven to 350°. Cream together the sugar and butter. Add eggs and milk and beat well. Sift together the flour, baking powder, cinnamon and nutmeg. Add to the egg mixture and mix well. Drop dates into a bag with 1/2 cup of flour in it and shake to coat the dates. Fold dates into the batter. Pour into two greased 8" cake pans and bake for 30 minutes, or until done.

## Maple Sponge Cake

| | | | | |
|---|---|---|---|---|
| 4 | egg whites | 1/2 | tea. baking powder |
| 1/4 | tea. salt | 4 | egg yolks |
| 3/4 | cup maple syrup | 1/2 | tea. vanilla |
| 1 | cup flour | | |

Preheat oven to 325°. Beat egg whites and salt until stiff. Heat syrup to boiling point and pour it very slowly over beaten egg whites, stirring constantly. Sift flour with baking powder and fold into syrup mixture. Beat egg yolks and vanilla until lemon colored and fold into mixture. Bake in ungreased tube pan for 50 minutes, or until done.

## Maple Spice Cake

| | | | | |
|---|---|---|---|---|
| 1/2 | cup shortening | 1 3/4 | cup flour |
| 3/4 | cup sugar | 2 | tea. baking powder |
| 1/4 | cup maple syrup | 1/2 | tea. salt |
| 2 | eggs, beaten | 1/2 | tea. cinnamon |
| 1/3 | cup milk | 1/4 tea. clove | |
| | | 1 | tea. vanilla |

Preheat oven to 350°. Cream shortening with sugar. Add in syrup and eggs; mix well. Add milk. Sift together flour, baking powder, salt, cinnamon and clove. Add to the mixture. Beat in vanilla. Pour batter into a greased 10" square cake pan. Cook for 40 minutes, or until done.

## Sour Cream Cake

| | | | | |
|---|---|---|---|---|
| 1 | egg, beaten | 1 1/2 | cups flour | |
| 1 | cup maple sugar | 1 | tea. baking soda | |
| 1 | cup sour cream | 1/2 | tea. salt | |
| | | 1 | tea. vanilla | |

Preheat oven to 350°. Add sugar to beaten egg and beat for one minute. Add sour cream alternately with flour which has been sifted with the baking soda and salt. Add vanilla and mix batter well. Pour into greased 9" cake pan and bake for 25 minutes, or until done. May be served warm or cooled to room temperature and frosted.

## Maple-Butterscotch Cake

| | | | | |
|---|---|---|---|---|
| 1/4 | cup soft butter | 1 | tea. baking powder | |
| 1 | cup maple sugar | 1/4 | tea. salt | |
| 1 | egg, beaten | 1 | tea. vanilla | |
| 1 | cup flour | 1/2 | cup chopped nuts | |

Preheat oven to 350°. Cream butter and sugar; add egg and mix well. Sift together flour, baking powder and salt and add to the mixture. Add vanilla and mix well. Stir in nuts. Spread in a greased 9" cake pan and bake for 25 minutes, or until done.

## Raisin-Applesauce Cake

2 1/2 cups flour  
1 1/2 tea. baking soda  
1 tea. salt  
1 tea. cinnamon  
1/2 tea. clove  
1/2 tea. nutmeg  

3/4 cup shortening  
1 1/4 cups sugar  
2 eggs, beaten  
1/2 cup maple syrup  
1 (17 oz.) can of applesauce  
1/2 cup chopped nuts  

Preheat oven to 350°. Sift flour with baking soda, salt and spices. Cream shortening and sugar together and beat until fluffy. Add eggs and syrup and beat thoroughly. Stir in applesauce and nuts. Gradually add sifted ingredients and mix well. Pour into two greased 8" round or square baking pans and bake for 20 minutes, or until done.

## Maple Upside-Down Cake

3 Tbs. butter  
1 cup maple sugar  
1 cup pineapple sections  
3 eggs, separated  
1 cup white sugar  

1/4 cup milk  
1 tea. lemon extract  
1 cup flour  
1/2 tea. salt  
1 1/2 tea. baking powder  

Preheat oven to 350°. Melt butter and pour into bottom of 8" cake pan. Sprinkle maple sugar evenly over butter; top with pineapple sections.

Beat the three egg yolks with sugar, add milk and lemon extract and mix well. Sift together flour, salt and baking powder and add to milk mixture; blend well. Beat the three egg whites until stiff and fold into batter. Pour the batter over top of pineapples. Bake for 45 minutes, or until done. Invert on large plate and serve warm.

## Maple Marshmallow Frosting

2    cups maple sugar
1    cup light cream

1/2   lb. shredded
       marshmallows

Heat maple sugar and cream until sugar is dissolved. Then boil without stirring to 238° on a candy thermometer. Remove from heat, add marshmallows and beat until of right consistency to spread on cake. Yields 3 cups of frosting

## Maple Icing

3/4   cup maple syrup
1/2   cup sugar

1    egg white, stiffly beaten
1    tea. vanilla

Boil syrup and sugar until it threads when dropped from the tip of spoon. Pour slowly into beaten egg white, beating constantly. Add vanilla Spread over cake after cooling to room temperature.

## Maple Hard Sauce Icing

1/3   cup butter
2    cups confectioner's sugar
2    Tbs. cooked black coffee

3    Tbs. maple syrup
3    Tbs. light cream

Cream butter with sugar and coffee. Add syrup and cream and mix well Beat until creamy. Frosts one cake or 1 1/2 dozen cupcakes.

## Oatmeal Sugar Cake

1/2 cups flour
  tea. baking soda
/4  tea. cinnamon
/2  tea. salt
  cup rolled oats

1 1/4 cups boiling water
1/2  cup soft butter
1/2  cup maple sugar
1/2  cup white sugar
2    eggs
1    tea. vanilla

Preheat oven to 350°. Sift together flour, baking soda, cinnamon and alt; set aside. Combine rolled oats and water; let stand 15 minutes. In a bowl eat butter, both sugars, eggs and vanilla until light in color. Stir in oat mixture nd the flour mixture; mix well. Pour into a greased 9" pan and bake for 45 ninutes, or until done.

## Maple Fudge Sauce

  cup white sugar
  cup maple syrup

1/4  cup water
1    Tbs. butter

Place all ingredients in a saucepan and boil until candy thermometer egisters 234°. Cool until warm to the touch; spoon over cut cake, pudding, or :e cream.

## Irish Whiskey Fruitcake

| | | | | |
|---|---|---|---|---|
| 3 | cups sifted flour | | 8 | ozs. mixed candied fruits, chopped |
| 1/2 | tea. baking powder | | | |
| 1/2 | tea. cinnamon | | 1/4 | cup candied cherries, chopped |
| 1 | cup butter | | | |
| 1 | cup maple sugar, packed | | 1 | tea. grated lemon rind |
| 6 | eggs | | 1 | cup blanched almonds, chopped |
| 1/3 | cup Irish whiskey | | | |
| 1/2 | lb. raisins | | 1/2 | cup Irish whiskey |
| 1/2 | lb. currants | | | |

Heat oven to 275°. Line a 9"x3" tube pan with heavy brown pape
grease paper well. Sift flour, baking powder, and cinnamon together. Crea.
butter with maple sugar until fluffy. Add eggs, one at a time, beating well aft
each addition. Add flour mixture and the 1/3 cup of whiskey; mix well. Fold .
remaining ingredients, except for the 1/2 cup whiskey; blend well. Turn into tl
tube pan and bake 3 hours, or until done. Remove from oven and brush with tl
1/2 cup whiskey and let cake cool in pan. Wrap tightly in aluminum foil or se
in an airtight container for up to a month before serving. When ready to serv
the following glaze may be brushed on the cake:

In a saucepan combine 1/4 cup maple sugar, 3 Tbs. light corn syrup and
Tbs. water. Bring slowly to a boil; boil 2 minutes. Remove from heat, ac
1 Tbs. of lemon juice and stir to blend well. Brush cake with glaze ar.
enjoy!

## Caramel Frosting

1/2   cup soft butter  
1   cup maple sugar, packed

1/3   cup milk  
1   lb. confectioners' sugar, sifted

Combine butter and maple sugar in a saucepan. Cook over medium heat, stirring constantly, until mixture bubbles. Cook 1 minute. Pour into a mixing bowl; cool 10 minutes; stir in milk; cool completely. Add confectioners' sugar gradually, beating constantly until smooth. Yields enough frosting to fill and frost two 9" layers.

## Burnt Sugar Frosting

1/3   cup maple sugar  
1/3   cup water  
1/2   cup soft butter

2   egg yolks  
1   lb. confectioners' sugar

Heat sugar in a heavy skillet over _low_ heat, until it melts and turns a golden brown. Add water, a small amount at a time, stirring constantly. Boil the syrup for 1 minute; cool. Cream butter; blend in egg yolks. Add confectioner's sugar alternately with syrup; beat well to blend. Yields enough frosting to fill and frost two 9" layers.

## American Fudge Cake

| | | | |
|---|---|---|---|
| 4 | sqs. unsweetened chocolate | 1/2 | tea. baking soda |
| 1 | Tbs. instant coffee | 1/4 | tea. salt |
| 1/2 | cup water | 1/2 | cup shortening |
| 1 | cup maple sugar, packed | 1 | cup white sugar |
| 2 1/2 | cups flour | 3 | eggs |
| 2 | tea. baking powder | 1 | cup milk |

Preheat oven to 350°. Combine first four ingredients in top of double boiler. Heat over hot, not boiling, water, stirring until chocolate is melted. Sift flour, baking powder, soda, and salt together. With electric beater beat shortening, sugar, and eggs at high speed for 3 minutes. Blend in chocolate mixture. Add flour mixture alternately with milk, at low speed. Pour into two 8" cake pans and bake 25 minutes, or until cake tests done.

## Raisin-Nut Spice Cake

| | | | |
|---|---|---|---|
| 2 1/3 | cups flour | 1/2 | cup shortening |
| 1 | cup white sugar | 2/3 | cup maple sugar, packed |
| 1 1/2 | tea. baking powder | 1 | cup buttermilk |
| 1/2 | tea. baking soda | 3 | eggs |
| 1/2 | tea. salt | 1/2 | cup chopped nuts |
| 1 | tea. cinnamon | 1/2 | cup chopped raisins |
| 1/2 | tea. cloves | | |

Preheat oven to 350°. Sift first 7 ingredients together into a mixing bowl. Add shortening, maple sugar and buttermilk. Beat 2 minutes at medium speed on electric mixer. Add eggs; beat another 2 minutes. Stir in nuts and raisins. Turn into 2 greased 9" cake pans and bake 30 minutes, or until cake is done.

# Christmas Fruitcake

| | | | |
|---|---|---|---|
| 3 1/2 | cups sifted flour | 4 | ozs. candied lemon peel |
| 1 1/4 | tea. baking powder | 4 | ozs. candied citron |
| 1 | tea. salt | 1 | Tbs. grated orange rind |
| 2 | tea. cinnamon | 1/2 | cup orange juice |
| 1/4 | tea. cloves | 1 | cup grape jelly |
| 1 1/4 | cup raisins | 1 1/2 | cups shortening |
| 1 | cup chopped nuts | 2 1/2 | cups maple sugar, packed |
| 12 | ozs. dried apricots, chopped | 5 | eggs |
| 8 | ozs. candied cherries, halved | | |

Heat oven to 300°. Line a 10"x4" tube pan with heavy brown paper; grease paper. Sift first 5 ingredients together. In another bowl combine the raisins, nuts, apricots, cherries, lemon peel, and citron; reserve. Beat orange rind, juice, and jelly together with a fork in a small bowl; reserve. Beat shortening, sugar, and eggs in a large bowl until fluffy. Add flour mixture alternately with reserved orange juice mixture. Stir in reserved fruit mixture. Turn batter into tube pan and bake 3 to 4 hours, testing for doneness after the third hour. Cover the cake with heavy brown paper during the last hour of baking to keep top from darkening too much. Cool cake; remove from pan. Store in a tightly covered container for up to a month to mellow flavors. This cake is wonderful for Christmas giving as it can be prepared several weeks in advance of wrapping or shipment.

## Maple Nut Cake

1/2 cup shortening
1/2 cup sugar
2 eggs, beaten
2 1/2 cups flour
2 1/2 tea. baking powder

1 tea. salt
1/2 cup milk mixed with 1/2 cup maple syrup
1/2 cup chopped nuts

Preheat oven to 350o. Cream shortening and sugar together. Add eggs and mix well. Sift together the flour, baking powder and salt. Add the flour mixture alternately with the milk mixture to the creamed shortening. Mix well. Stir in nuts. Pour into greased tube pan. Bake for 50 minutes, or until done. May be iced or served plain.

## Maple-Apple Cake

4 apples, peeled and sliced
3/4 cup maple syrup
2 1/2 cups flour
1/2 tea. salt
1 1/2 tea. baking soda

1 tea. cinnamon
1/4 tea. _each:_ nutmeg, cloves, allspice
1/2 cup water
1/3 cup melted butter
1 egg, beaten

Preheat oven to 375°. Cook apple slices in the syrup over low heat until they are tender; cool to room temperature. Sift flour with salt, baking soda and spices. Combine water with the melted butter and stir into the sifted ingredients. Add the apple mixture and mix well. Stir in the egg. Pour into a greased 9''x11' pan. Bake for 30 minutes, or until done.

### Boiled Maple Cake*

| | | | |
|---|---|---|---|
| 1 | cup maple syrup | 1 | tea. <u>each:</u> cloves, nutmeg, cinnamon, salt |
| 1/2 | cup shortening | | |
| 1 | cup raisins | 1 | tea. baking soda |
| 1 | cup cold water | 1/2 | cup chopped nuts |
| 2 | cups flour | | |

Preheat oven to 350°. Boil syrup, shortening, raisins and cold water for 4 minutes. Remove from heat and chill for one hour. Sift together flour, spices and baking soda. Add to chilled mixture and beat well. Add nuts. Bake in a loaf pan for 1 hour, or until done.

### Maple Zuppa Inglese

| | | |
|---|---|---|
| 1 | package yellow cake mix | 1 1/3 cups maple syrup |
| 1/2 | package instant vanilla pudding | 1 1/3 cups rum |
| | | whipped cream |

Prepare the yellow cake mix in two layers, following package directions. Let stand, uncovered, for several hours. Prepare the 1/2 package of pudding mix and chill while cake is standing. When cake has stood long enough mix the syrup and rum together. Pour 1/2 of the mixture over each layer. Let stand for 20 minutes. Put layers together with pudding in between. Top with whipped cream and serve immediately.

# Pies

*Pies, puddings, and pancakes are the best with sweetening,
and as sugar is as cheap and agreeable an article as we can find,
we had better be attending to our caldrons.
Heaven has been extremely propitious to our country in causing the
growth of this valuable tree: the maple.*

Farmer's Almanac, 1808

## Maple Custard Pie

| | | | |
|---|---|---|---|
| 3 | cups milk | 1/4 | tea. salt |
| 3 | egg yolks, beaten | 3 | egg whites, stiffly beaten |
| 1 | cup maple syrup | 1 | tea. vanilla |
| 1/4 | cup sugar | 1 | uncooked 10" pie shell |
| 1 | Tbs. flour | | |

Preheat oven to 325°. Scald milk. Add to it the egg yolks, syrup, sugar, flour and salt. Continue cooking mixture slowly until it begins to thicken. Remove from heat and fold in the egg whites and vanilla. Pour into pie shell and bake 30 minutes, or until custard is firm. May be served at room temperature or chilled.

## Maple Squash Pie

| | | | |
|---|---|---|---|
| 1 | cup smooth squash | 1/4 | tea. ginger |
| 1/2 | cup maple syrup | 1 | tea. cinnamon |
| 1 | egg, beaten | 1 | scant cup of milk |
| 1/2 | tea. salt | 1 | unbaked 9" pie shell |

Preheat oven to 450°. Mix squash, syrup, egg, salt and spices together well. Add milk gradually, stirring slowly. Fill pie shell and bake for 10 minutes at 450°; reduce temperature to 350° and cook for an additional 40 minutes, or until done. May be served at room temperature or chilled.

## Deep Dish Apple Pie

| | | | |
|---|---|---|---|
| 6 | apples | 1/2 | tea. cinnamon |
| 1 | cup maple sugar | 1/2 | tea. salt |
| 2 | Tbs. flour | 1 | Tbs. butter |
| | | Pastry for 1 crust | |

*Preheat oven to 375°. Pare the apples and slice them very thin. Put the apples in a large bowl and add maple sugar, flour, cinnamon and salt. Mix well to coat all of apples. Place them in a 2 to 3 quart buttered casserole, dot with butter and cover with piecrust dough. Bake for one hour, or until brown and bubbly. Serve warm. Serves 6. May be topped with whipped cream, or cheese if you prefer.*

## Fresh Peach Pie

| | | | |
|---|---|---|---|
| 4 | cups sliced fresh peaches | 1/4 | tea. salt |
| 1 | cup maple sugar | 2 | Tbs butter |
| 1/2 | tea. cinnamon | Pastry for a 2-crust pie | |
| 4 | Tbs. flour | | |

*Preheat oven to 425°. Put peaches in a large bowl; add sugar, cinnamon, flour and salt and mix to coat peaches well. Fill pastry-lined 9" pie plate with peaches and dot with butter. Cover with upper crust. Bake for 50 minutes, or until done. Serve warm.*

## Maple Apple Pie

| | | | |
|---|---|---|---|
| 4 | cups of apples, peeled and sliced thinly | 1/4 | tea. cinnamon |
| 1 | cup maple sugar | 1 | Tbs. flour |
| 1/4 | tea. salt | 2 | Tbs. butter |
| | | | Pastry for a 2-crust pie |

Preheat oven to 450°. Line a 9" pie plate with pastry crust and put in the apples. In a bowl combine the sugar, salt, cinnamon and flour; sprinkle mixture over apples. Dot with butter. Cover with top crust and cut air vents. Bake in a 450° oven for 10 minutes and then reduce heat to 350° and bake 40 minutes, or until done. May be served warm or at room temperature. Top with a slice of cheese if you desire for a special New England treat.

## Maple Cream Pie

| | | | |
|---|---|---|---|
| 1 | pint milk, scalded | 2 | eggs, beaten |
| 1 | cup maple sugar | 1/2 | tea. salt |
| 3 | Tbs. cornstarch | 1 | Tbs. butter |
| 1/4 | cup milk | 1 | tea. vanilla |
| | | 1 | baked 9" pie shell |

Put the pint of milk and maple sugar in the top of double boiler and heat until sugar is dissolved. Add the cornstarch to the 1/4 cup milk and stir until dissolved. Add this milk mixture to the double boiler and cook for 1/2 hour on low heat, stirring occasionally. Add the hot mixture to the eggs, stir, and return to the double boiler; cook for one minute. Remove from heat, add salt, butter and vanilla. Cool to room temperature. Pour into the baked pie shell. May be served immediately or chilled.

## Brandy Mincemeat Pie

| | | | |
|---|---|---|---|
| 3 | cups prepared mincemeat | | Enough piecrust dough for a |
| 1 1/2 | cups chopped walnuts | | two-crust pie |
| 1/2 | cup maple sugar, packed | 4 | Tbs. soft butter |
| 1/2 | cup brandy | 1 | Tbs. light cream |

_The night before:_ Combine mincemeat, walnuts, maple sugar and brandy. Refrigerate to allow the flavors to blend. (This can be done as far ahead as two days in advance.) Roll out each piecrust separately, brush with 2 Tbs. of butter each, fold in half and refrigerate an hour.

Preheat oven to 425°. Roll out bottom crust of pie, fit into pie plate, and fill with mincemeat mixture (undrained). Adjust top crust and brush with the light cream. Bake for 30 minutes, or until nicely browned. Serve warm.

## Wonderful Walnut Pie

| | | | |
|---|---|---|---|
| Unbaked 9" Pie Shell | | 1/4 | cup maple syrup |
| 1/2 | cup maple sugar, packed | 1/2 | cup milk |
| 1/2 | cup soft butter | 1 | cup chopped walnuts |
| 3/4 | cup white sugar | 1/2 | tea. vanilla |
| 3 | eggs | 1/4 | cup broken walnuts |
| 1/4 | tea. salt | whipped cream (optional) | |

Preheat oven to 350°. In double boiler top, with electric mixer, mix maple sugar and butter until well blended. Add white sugar and mix well. Add eggs, one at a time, beating constantly. Add salt, maple syrup, milk, and mix well.

Cook, over boiling water, for 5 minutes, stirring constantly. Remove from heat and stir in the 1 cup of chopped walnuts. Add vanilla. Pour into the unbaked pie shell. Bake for one hour, scatter the broken walnuts over the top, and bake for 5 minutes more. Cool before serving.

## Maple Sugar Pie

| | | | |
|---|---|---|---|
| 2 | egg yolks | 2 | cups milk |
| 1 | cup maple syrup | 1 | tea. vanilla |
| dash | of salt | 1 | Tbs. butter |
| 2 | Tbs. cornstarch | 1 | _baked_ 9" pie shell |

Beat egg yolks and stir in maple syrup. Add salt and cornstarch to the mixture and stir well. Put milk into top of double boiler and heat to almost boiling. Add mixture to milk and cook slowly, covered, until it thickens. Remove from heat and add vanilla and butter and mix well. Pour into cooked pie shell and chill before cutting.

## Maple Chiffon Pie

| | | | |
|---|---|---|---|
| 1 | Tbs. plain gelatin | 2 | egg yolks, beaten |
| 3 | Tbs. cold water | 2 | egg whites, beaten |
| 1/2 | cup milk | 1 | cup heavy cream, whipped |
| 1/2 | cup maple syrup | | with 1 tea. vanilla |
| 1/2 | tea. salt | 1 | _baked_ 9" pie shell |

Soak gelatin in the cold water. Heat milk, syrup and salt in top of double boiler until hot and well mixed. Slowly pour the hot mixtuer over the beaten egg yolks in a bowl and stir. Return all of mixture to double boiler; add soaked gelatin and cook slowly, covered, until it thickens; stir occasionally. Remove from heat and chill for one hour. Fold in beaten egg whites and 1/2 of the whipped cream. Pour into the baked pie shell and chill. Top with remaining whipped cream when ready to serve.

## Maple Nut Pie

| | | | |
|---|---|---|---|
| 1 | cup milk | 1 | Tbs. cornstarch |
| 1 | cup maple syrup | pinch | of salt |
| 1 | Tbs. butter | 3/4 | cup chopped nuts |
| 3 | egg yolks, beaten | | whipped cream ( for topping) |
| 1 | Tbs. flour | 1 | _baked_ 9" pie shell |

Place milk and syrup in top of double boiler and cook slowly until hot and well mixed. (Milk will give the appearance of looking sour, but it's not.) Remove from heat and add butter and egg yolks and mix well. Stir in flour, cornstarch and salt. Return to double boiler and cook slowly until thick; add nuts. Cool to almost room temperature. Pour into pie crust. Chill and top with whipped cream when ready to serve.

## Maple Pumpkin Pie

| | | | |
|---|---|---|---|
| 1 | cup smooth pumpkin | 1/2 | cup milk |
| 1 | Tbs. cornstarch | 1 1/3 | cups maple syrup |
| 1/2 | tea. nutmeg | 2 | beaten eggs |
| 1/4 | tea. salt | 1 | _uncooked_ 10" pie shell |
| 1 | Tbs. melted butter | | |

Preheat oven to $450^o$. In a large mixing bowl thoroughly mix pumpkin with cornstarch, nutmeg and salt. Then add butter, milk and syrup. Mix well. Stir in beaten eggs. Pour into pie shell and bake at $450^o$ for 15 minutes; reduce the oven to $325^o$ and cook for 40 minutes, or until done. Cool to room temperature before serving.

# Desserts

*There is now more reason than ever*
*for attending to making sugar from the maple tree,*
*as we are now deprived from obtaining it abroad because of the War of 1812.*
*Those, therefore, who have the means will not neglect*
*to manufacture this all-important article.*

*Farmer's Almanac, 1814*

## Pear Butterscotch Crisp

| | | | | |
|---|---|---|---|---|
| 1 | 2-pound can of pear halves, drained | | 1/4 | tea. salt |
| 1/2 | cup maple sugar, packed | | 1/4 | tea. cinnamon |
| 1/2 | cup flour | | 1/4 | cup butter |

Preheat oven to 425°. Put pear halves, cut sides down, in a greased pie plate. Mix sugar, flour, salt and cinnamon; with a fork work in butter until crumbly. Sprinkle over and around pears. Bake 15 minutes, or until crumbs are golden brown. Serve warm. Makes 4 servings.

## Apple Tapioca Surprise

| | | | | |
|---|---|---|---|---|
| 3 | apples, peeled and sliced | | 1 | cup maple sugar, packed |
| 2 | Tbs. butter | | 3/4 | tea. salt |
| 1 | tea. mace | | 2 | Tbs. lemon juice |
| 1/3 | cup quick-cooking tapioca | | 2 1/4 | cups water |

Preheat oven to 375°. Arrange apple slices evenly in a 9"x9"x2" baking dish. Dot with butter and sprinkle with mace.

In a saucepan combine the tapioca, maple sugar, salt, lemon juice, and water; bring to a boil, while stirring.

Pour the tapioca mixture over the apple slices and bake for 20 minutes, or until done. Serve warm. Makes 6 servings.

## Butterscotch Brownies

| | | | | |
|---|---|---|---|---|
| 1/3 | cup butter | | 1/4 | tea. salt |
| 1 | cup maple sugar | | 1 | tea. baking powder |
| 1 | egg | | 1 | cup flour |
| 1/2 | cup chopped nuts | | 1 | tea. vanilla |

Preheat oven to 350°. Melt butter. Add rest of ingredients and mix well. Spread thinly on a greased 8"x8"x2" pan. Bake 20 minutes, or until done. Yields 9-12 brownies.

## Peanut Apple Crisp

| | | | | |
|---|---|---|---|---|
| 3 | cups apples, peeled and sliced | | 3 | Tbs. flour |
| 1/3 | cup water | | 3/4 | cup oatmeal |
| 1/4 | cup maple syrup | | 1/4 | cup maple sugar |
| juice | of 1/2 lemon | | 1/3 | cup peanut butter |
| 3/4 | tea. cinnamon | | 2 | Tbs. butter |

Preheat oven to 350°. Place apples in a 2 to 3 quart baking dish, greased. Mix water, maple syrup, lemon and cinnamon together and pour over apples. Mix together flour, oatmeal, sugar, peanut butter and butter thoroughly. Sprinkle over cinnamon mixture. Bake for 50 minutes, or until done. Serve with whipped cream if you desire.

## Frozen Maple Parfait

| | |
|---|---|
| 3/4 | cup maple syrup |
| 3 | eggs, separated |
| 1 1/2 | cups heavy cream, whipped |

| | |
|---|---|
| 1 | tea. vanilla |
| 1/8 | tea. salt, added before egg whites are beaten |

Heat syrup to boiling point in top of double boiler. Pour syrup slowly over beaten egg yolks and return to top of double boiler. Over low heat beat the mixture until it is thick and light in color. Pour it over stiffly beaten egg whites and stir. Chill for one hour. Add whipped cream and vanilla. Pour into ice cube trays (without cube separators) and freeze without stirring. Serves 6.

## Maple Coconut Squares

| | |
|---|---|
| 1/2 | cup butter, soft |
| 1 | cup flour |
| 1 | cup maple sugar |
| 1 | cup shredded coconut |

| | |
|---|---|
| 1/2 | cup chopped nuts |
| 2 | eggs, beaten |
| 6 | tea. flour |
| 1/2 | tea. baking powder |

Preheat oven to 375°. Cut butter into flour as you would for pie crust. Pat it into an 8" square pan and bake for 12 minutes. Mix other ingredients together well and spread over cooked layer. Return to oven and bake 30 minutes reducing heat to 350°. Cool and cut into squares. Yields 9-12 squares.

## Maple Cupcakes

| | | | |
|---|---|---|---|
| 1/4 | cup soft butter | 1 1/2 | cups flour |
| 1/2 | cup maple sugar | 2 1/2 | tea. baking powder |
| 1 | egg, beaten | 1/2 | tea. salt |
| | | 1/2 | cup milk |

*Preheat oven to 400°. Cream together the butter, maple sugar and egg. Sift together the flour, baking powder and salt. Add to first mixture alternately with the 1/2 cup of milk. Mix well and pour into greased cupcake tins. Bake for 15 minutes, or until done. Yields 1 dozen.*

## Apple-Maple Cobbler

| | | | |
|---|---|---|---|
| 3/4 | cup maple syrup | 1/2 | cup sugar |
| 1/2 | cup boiling water | 1 1/2 | cups sifted flour |
| 1 | tea. vanilla | 1 | tea. baking powder |
| 2 | apples, peeled and sliced | 1/4 | tea. salt |
| 2 | Tbs. soft butter | 1/2 | cup milk |

*Preheat oven to 375°. Combine maple syrup with the water and reheat to boiling, add vanilla and simmer on lowest heat while preparing apples and batter. Put apple slices into bottom of buttered 7"x10" baking pan. Cream butter and sugar. Sift flour, baking powder and salt together. Add the dry ingredients to the creamed butter; add milk and mix together well. Spread this thick batter over apple slices and then pour the simmering syrup evenly over the batter. Bake for 40 minutes, or until done. Serve warm. Serves 6-8.*

## Maple Gingerbread*

| | | | |
|---|---|---|---|
| 1/4 | cup shortening | Sift together: | |
| 1/2 | cup maple syrup | 1 | tea. ginger |
| 1/2 | cup brown sugar | 1/4 | tea. salt |
| 3/4 | cup sour milk | 2 | cups flour |
| 2 | eggs, beaten | 1 | tea. baking soda |

Preheat oven to 350°. In a saucepan, on low heat, warm shortening, syrup and sugar until dissolved. Remove from heat. Add sour milk and eggs. Add sifted ingredients and beat mix well. Pour into 9" square pan. Bake 25-30 minutes, or until done.

## Maple Meringue Squares

| | | | |
|---|---|---|---|
| 1/4 | cup butter | 1/4 | tea. salt |
| 1/2 | cup white sugar | 1 | tea. vanilla |
| 1 | egg, separated | 1/2 | cup chopped nuts |
| 3/4 | cup flour | 1 | cup maple sugar |
| 1/2 | tea. baking powder | | |

Preheat oven to 350°. Cream together the butter, white sugar and egg yolk. Sift together flour, baking powder and salt. Add to creamed mixture and mix well. Add vanilla.

In a greased 10" cake pan spread the batter 1/4" thick. Sprinkle with nuts. Beat egg white until stiff and fold it into the maple sugar. Pour slowly over batter mixture and spread evenly. Bake for 30 minutes, or until done. Cool and cut into squares. Yields 9-12 squares.

## Maple Baked Peaches

| | | |
|---|---|---|
| 4 | fresh peaches | whipped cream |
| 1/2 | cup maple syrup | |

Preheat oven to 350°. Peel peaches and cut in half; remove pits. Place in a glass baking dish and cover with syrup. Bake peaches until tender when pierced with a fork. Serve warm with whipped cream. Serves 4.

## Maple Oatmeal Bars*

| | | | | |
|---|---|---|---|---|
| 1/2 | cup softened shortening | | scant tea. baking powder |
| 1/2 | cup sugar | | 1/2 | tea. salt |
| 1/2 | cup maple syrup | | 1/2 | cup chopped nuts |
| 1 | egg, beaten | | 1 | cup oatmeal (quick |
| 1 | tea. vanilla | | | cooking |
| 2/3 | cup flour | | | |

Preheat oven to 350°. Cream shortening and sugar; stir in syrup, egg and vanilla. Sift together the flour, baking powder and salt; stir in nuts and add to the syrup batter. Mix well. Stir in the oatmeal. Spread in a greased 9" square pan. Bake for 35 minutes, or until done. Cut squares while still warm. Yields 9-12 squares.

# Mixed Drinks

Judge E. Speer, of the southern district of Georgia, had before his court a typical charge of illicit distilling. "What's your name?" demanded the Judge.

"Joshua," drawled the prisoner.

"Joshua—the man who made the sun stand still?" smiled the Judge, in amusement at the laconic answer.

"No, sir; Joshua who made the moon shine!" answered the quick-witted mountaineer.

*Farmer's Almanac*

## Hot Maple Rum

| | | | |
|---|---|---|---|
| 4 | ozs. rum | | juice of two lemons |
| 2 | Tbs. maple syrup | | hot water |

Stir together the rum, syrup and juice of lemons until well blended. Pour half of mixture into each of two 10 oz. glasses. Fill glasses with hottest tap water and stir. Serves 2.

## Mint Julep

| | | | |
|---|---|---|---|
| 8 | sprigs of mint | 2 | dashes of bitters |
| 4 | tea. maple syrup | 4 | jiggers of whiskey |

Crush mint and add the maple syrup. Stir well. Add bitters and whiskey; stir well. Fill 2 glasses with shaved ice and pour mixture in. Serves 2.

## Old Fashioned

| | | | |
|---|---|---|---|
| 2 | jiggers of whiskey | 2 | tea. maple syrup |
| 4 | dashes of bitters | 2 | tea. cherry juice |

Shake all ingredients well and pour into 2 glasses filled with ice cubes. Serves 2.

## Whiskey Sour

| 4 | Tbs. maple syrup | 3 | jiggers of whiskey |
|---|---|---|---|
| juice of 1 lemon | | 1/2 | cup soda water |
| juice of 1 orange | | | |

Shake all ingredients well with shaved ice and strain into two tall glasses. Serves 2.

## Bourbon Fizz

| 2 | oz. bourbon | juice of 1 lemon |
|---|---|---|
| 2 | tea. maple syrup | |

Shake all ingredients well. Pour into 2 glasses and add ice cubes. Serves 2

## Apple Rabbit

| 3 | jiggers apple brandy | 1 | jigger orange juice |
|---|---|---|---|
| 1 | jigger lemon juice | | maple syrup to taste |

Shake brandy, lemon juice and orange juice well in shaved ice. Add maple syrup to suit your taste. Shake well. Strain into 3 glasses. Serves 3.

# Miscellaneous

## RECIPE TO KEEP ONE'S SELF WARM A WHOLE WINTER WITH ONE PIECE OF WOOD

Take a piece of wood, fling it out the window into the Yard; then run downstairs as hard as you ever can; when you have got it, run up again with the same measure of speed; keep throwing and fetching up until the Exercise shall have sufficiently heated you. Renew as often as the occasion shall require!

*Farmer's Almanac, 1784*

## Maple Sugar Sauce

| | | | |
|---|---|---|---|
| 1 1/2 | cups maple sugar | 2 | tea. vanilla |
| 1/2 | cup light cream | 1 | Tbs. butter |

Cook sugar and cream on low heat until mixture bubbles. Add vanilla and butter and beat until thick. Serve warm over ice cream or pudding.

## Maple Marinade

| | | | |
|---|---|---|---|
| 1/4 | cup soy sauce | 2 | Tbs. oil |
| 1/4 | cup orange juice | 2 | Tbs. minced onion |
| 1/4 | cup lemon juice | 1 | crushed clove garlic |
| 2 | Tbs. maple sugar | salt and pepper | |

This marinade is good for 2 pounds of lamb, chicken, beef or pork. Simply mix the ingredients together, add meat, and refrigerate for 2 hours. Meat can then be oven-baked or barbequed. Baste with the marinade as it is cooking

## Fruit Salad Dressing

| | | | |
|---|---|---|---|
| | egg yolk, beaten | 2 | Tbs. Lemon juice |
| 4 | cup maple syrup | 1/4 | cup whipped cream |

Place egg yolk and maple syrup into a double boiler and cook for 1 minute, *irring*. Cool to room temperature. Fold in lemon juice and whipped cream. *>oon* over fruit salad.

## Maple Milkshake*

For each milkshake stir 2 Tbs. of maple syrup into one cup of milk. Add a *:oop* of vanilla ice cream and mix well in blender.

## Haymaker's Switchel

| | | | |
|---|---|---|---|
| | cup brown sugar | 3/4 | cup of red cider vinegar |
| | quarts water | 1/2 | tea. ginger |
| /2 | cup maple syrup | | |

Mix all ingredients in a large pitcher and stir until well blended. Refrigerate *intil* switchel is just cool. Serves 5 cups.

### Homemade Maple Syrup*

Boil whatever amount of sap you have to 7° above the boiling point of water as registered by your candy thermometer; bottle and seal. Canning jars or plastic bottles serve equally well. Should mold form after a period of time simply reheat syrup to 180° and skim off impurities. Opened syrup should be refrigerated.

### Maple Cream*

Fancy or Grade A maple syrup is recommended for a delicious and light maple cream. One pint of syrup yields almost a pint of cream.

Cook whatever amount of syrup you have to 20° above the boiling point of water as registered by your candy thermometer. Remove from heat and cool to room temperature. Stir with a wooden spoon until cream becomes light. Store in airtight plastic or glass containers to keep fresh. Cream is delicious on hot toast, pancakes, English muffins, or donuts.

### Sugar on Snow*

Boil a pint of maple syrup until it reaches 232° on a candy thermometer. Drop by small spoonfuls on top of dishes hardpacked with snow. Eat with a spoon. Add some plain donuts and sour pickles for a complete winter party.

## Spareribs with Maple Sauce

| | | | |
|---|---|---|---|
| 1/2 | cups maple syrup | 1 | tea. salt |
| | Tbs. chili sauce | 1/2 | tea. dry mustard |
| | Tbs. cider vinegar | 1/2 | tea. pepper |
| 1/2 | Tbs. chopped onion | 3 | pounds spareribs, cut in |
| | Tbs. Worcestershire sauce | | 4" pieces |

Preheat oven to 350°. Combine all ingredients, except spareribs, in a bowl nd mix well. Brush sauce on spareribs and put them in a single layer in a allow roasting pan. Do not cover. Roast about 1 1/2 hours, brushing frequently ith sauce. Turn occasionally for an even glaze. Serves 4.

## Banana Eggnog

Peel a ripe banana and cut into small pieces. Blend in electric blender with egg, 2 Tbs. maple syrup and one cup of milk. Serves 2.

## Tasty Pot Roast

For a change of taste in your pot roast, rub the sides of the meat with 2 ˉbs. of maple sugar, 1/4 cup flour, 1 tea. salt and 1/2 tea. dry mustard before rowning meat in fat. Then proceed as usual.

## Some Other Delicious Ways to Use
### Maple Products

*Children love a tablespoon of syrup stirred into their milk.*

*Drizzle syrup over hot cereal or grapefruit.*

*Warmed syrup over vanilla ice cream with nuts makes a great sundae*

*Baked apples are delicious when syrup is poured into cored-out center just before baking.*

*A tablespoon of syrup stirred into a glass of ginger ale is a very old New England treat for young and old alike.*

*Baste ham or ham slices with syrup while baking or frying.*

*Add 1/2 cup of syrup for each pound of beans you are baking, in place of molasses.*

*Sprinkle maple sugar instead of white sugar when making cinnamon toast*

*A maple cream and peanut butter sandwich is delicious!*

# Index